P9-BIN-748

This book is for the babysitters all over the world who care for our little ones, and is dedicated to my dear friends Eroca and Kris, who are always there for our kitties.

Copyright © 2010 by Pam Choi. All rights reserved.
Published by Faux Paw Media Group, A Division of Faux Paw Productions, Inc.™
www.fauxpawproductions.com

This book may not be reproduced in whole or in part, by any means (with the exception of short quotes for the purpose of review), without the expressed written permission of the publisher,
Faux Paw Media Group, 718 Cliff Drive
Laguna Beach, California 92651 USA

.

Composed in the United States of America
First Imprint 2010
Bart Gets a Babysitter ©
ISBN 978-1-935824-93-0
SAN:850-637X

Library of Congress Cataloging –in-Publication Data
Bart Gets a Babysitter is composed and written by Pam Choi
Summary: Bart is both anxious and excited to have a babysitter stay with him
[1.Cats-fiction. 2. Pets-fiction. 3. Family-fiction. 4. Home-fiction 5. Babysitter-fiction]
I. Title II. Choi, Pam

Bart Gets a Babysitter

by Pam Choi

Hi! My name is Bart...

... Bart the Cat.

I consider myself a cat of adventure and I have many tales to tell.

This tale is about my babysitter, Eroca.

Mom told me that she and Dad were going to visit my Aunt Penny in North Carolina.

Oh my!

That sounds far away.

What about me?

Mom picked me up and pet me softly.

"Don't worry Bart," she told me, "You are going to have a babysitter."

What's a babysitter, I wondered.

My Dad sat down and put me on his lap.

He told me a babysitter takes care of you when you are too young to be alone.

Dad said my babysitter's name was Eroca.

He told me that she would take very good care of me and that she would be very nice to me.

I wonder if she likes to play games!

**Maybe I can be a babysitter someday!
What an adventure that would be!**

On the day my Mom and Dad were leaving, I waited in my basket by the door for Eroca...

... and I waited.

And I waited some more.

Then the doorbell rang!

I was not sure if I should be nervous or excited.

When she walked in, I knew it was going to be okay.

She had a very friendly smile.

When Mom introduced us, Eroca sat down on the floor!

Now we were the same size!
Well, almost.

She slowly put her hand out for me to smell.

She smelled nice.

Eroca told me all about herself and how much she likes animals.

She has a cat and a dog at her house. Their names are Clara Bell and Lido. Maybe I will meet them someday.

We could go on an adventure together!

My Mom and Dad said goodbye and told me they would be home soon.

I was a little sad, but I always try to be brave and I have my new friend Eroca to take care of me.

I have a new friend!

I love making new friends!

Eroca and I had fun playing games and she gave me my food at dinnertime.

We had a great day together.

Guess what?

I hear Eroca calling me.

She says it's time for bed.

I am ready to go to sleep.
We had a busy day.

Tonight I will dream about my babysitter and all of my friends and family.

I hope you have nice dreams of friends and family too.

Until next time...

... Bart the Cat.

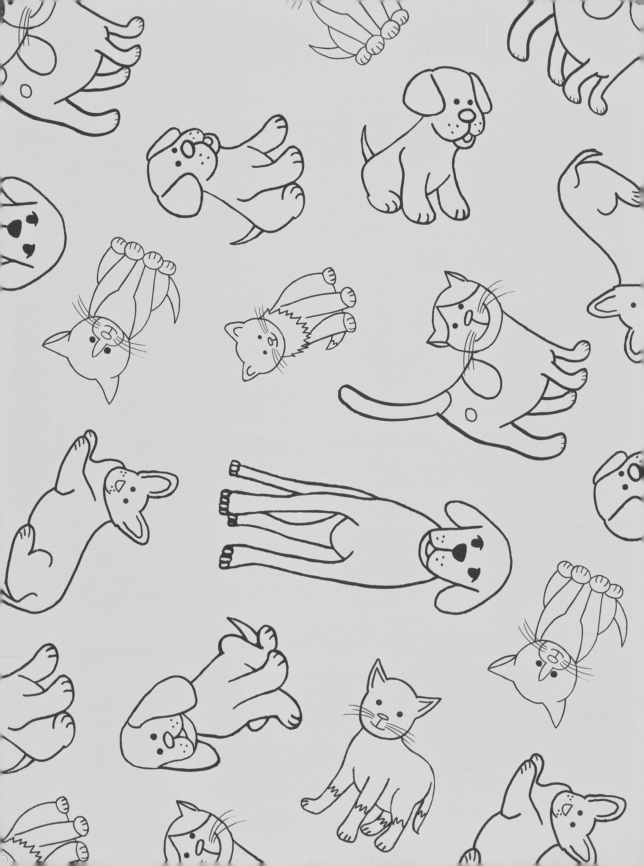